MUSINGS OF A MUSE

MUCH COGITATED THOUGHTS

DR. SUMAN KUMAR KASTURI

Dedicated to my wife

Uma Rani Kasturi

Contents

Preface

The intellectual is constantly betrayed by his vanity. Godlike he blandly assumes that he can express everything in words whereas the things one loves, lives, and dies for are not, in the last analysis completely expressible in words.

— Anne Morrow Lindbergh

Life is a continuous chain of experiences. These experiences are both good and bad but both help us live a more educated and productive life. Nonetheless, it is practically not possible to experience everything in the ephemeral life. Yet, it is possible to get second-hand experiences inspired by the lives of others. Yes, it is been inside all of us — the power of observing things. But, what differs from a person to person is — the confidence, talent and the ability to pen down those observations. This book, "The Musings of a Muse: Much Cogitated Thoughts," is an anthology of the thoughts — an inspiration drawn by the author from so many facets of his life!

Acknowledgements

"Gratitude will shift you to a higher frequency, and you will attract much better things."– Rhonda Byrne

When the acknowledgements are meant for a book that is purely based on frequencies and frequency bands, I thought that there is no better opening than the above quote by Rhonda Byrne. Indeed, I second this thought that gratitude will swing to a higher rate of recurrence for enticing much better things!

Profoundly, the roots of all goodness lie in the soil of appreciation for goodness. Irrefutably, I have drawn inspiration from many people in my life. For this reason and beyond, when I am about to give rise to salutations, I made it certain to be very genuine in expressing my gratitude to the most deserving people in my life.

When I read the following words of Ezra Taft Benson for the first time, I felt that he had experienced and expressed a similar responsive state of mine. The words that I am referring here are:

Our parents deserve our honour and respect for giving us life itself. Beyond this, they almost always made countless sacrifices as they cared for and nurtured us through our infancy and childhood, provided us with the necessities of life, and nursed us through physical illnesses and the emotional stresses of growing up.

There are no second thoughts for me that predominantly I would like to express my earnest gratitude to my parents — (Late) Kasturi Sreeramaiah and Kasturi Savitha for their eternal love. The only person in my life whom I have given the matching position to that of my parents is my wife — Uma Rani Kasturi; she has been so caring and special for me.

In essence, I owe so much to all my teachers — (Late) R.J. Prasad, Raja Rao, Charles, Purnachander Rao, Padma Kumar, Madhava Reddy, Raju, M. Suresh, Fr. Antony, Fr. Jnanadevan, Fr. Elias, Fr. Alphonsus, and Fr. Marianna (my teachers at St Xavier's High School, Suryapet); Pushpanathan, (Late) Fr. Mathews and Fr. Dhan Paul (my teachers at Loyola Academy, Secunderabad), from whom I have learnt many things — both academic and non-academic. This list would be incomplete without mentioning about my research guide Prof. Amancherla Subrahmanyam (Founder Registrar of Damodaram Sanjeevaiah National Law University & former Dean of PG Department of Legal Studies at Acharya Nagarjuna University). He was not only a research guide for my PhD but also an interminable spring of moral support. I wish I would be at least half of what he has been to me and the rest of his students if I ever take an academic path.

Certainly, I give due credit to the Indian Air Force for what I am today. I am indebted to my colleagues at Indian Air Force, who have extended great support during my Air Force years and even after that. They have always been there for me in times of need and deed. There are many people I am indebted to — too numerous to name. Nonetheless, I would like to especially convey my sincere gratitude to Ankireddipalli Venugopal Reddy and Vangapandu Yuga Satya Murthy for their back-up and prop up.

I would also like to express my sincere thanks to all my family members — Late Dr Karli Vittal, Karli Aruna (Laxmi Rajyam); Dontha Venkateswara Prasad, Dontha Hari Ranjani; Punna Prasad, Punna Lakshmi Niveditha; and Karli Vijay Prakash, Karli Nirmala.

I also extend my sincere thanks to Prof C. Pichandy (Former HoD & Professor at PSG College of Arts and Science, Coimbatore), Prof Sunil Kanta Behera (Professor of Eminence at Tezpur University), Prof P. Bobby Vardhan (Professor at Andhra University), Babji Yana (National Secretary General, PRSI and Editor PR Voice) for their support and encouragement.

Finally, this book would have not been possible without the support and sacrifice of my children — Kasturi Sai Advait & Kasturi Sai Advik. They have been willing to help me by sacrificing their authentic rights and making easy for me to complete this project in time. Before I settle, I would like to once again thank my perfect wife — Uma Rani Kasturi, for everything! Without her priceless support and sacrifice, this work would have never been achievable!!

-Dr Suman Kumar Kasturi

CHAPTER ONE

Musings 1

"It is better to stand up for one's own beliefs and get kicked in the shin rather than lie down and get hit on the face"

"As a child, everyone wants to grow up fast; and when grow up, everyone wants to go back to their childhood days!"

"In life, certain things do change but remain the same!"

"No side of the war is ever prepared to risk retribution against its population. Then why shouldn't there be adequate efforts to prevent conflict?"

"Mere living and life aren't the same! "

"They say that the Internet is the eighth wonder. Nonetheless, I consider it as the only wonder!"

"In situations wherein the word of mouth fail, music plays a significant role in expressing aesthetics!"

◆

"In seclusion, I become an ardent votary of Goddess Saraswati (Apollo)!"

◆

"History should never be viewed as the actual version of incidents ...rather it should be viewed only as of the opinion of the historian!"

◆

"I believe that a good book has more gravity than the earth!"

◆

"A warrior who cannot show fortitude is not less than any coward!"

◆

"Social Media is the conglomeration of people with heterodox opinions, often taken advantage of by the Artificial Intelligence!"

◆

"Fooling others is also an art that everyone cannot master!"

◆

"Many recondite innovations initially seem abysmal, before they deliver results!"

◆

"Indubitably, newspapers have been mired and become lackadaisical due to the magnificent play of the new media!"

◆

"Post-retirement period should be the chapter of a sempiternal tour of wisdom!"

◆

"Most of the happenings in the contemporary society are Social Media's gambit for attracting attention!"

◈

"Almost every Indian is knackered with the present-day politics!"

◈

"Social Media has become a platform for opponents to generate a steady stream of billingsgate!"

◈

"No proper reflection can be obtained from the mirror that shakes. Similarly, no proper decision can be taken by the mind that wavers from its focal point!"

◈

"Human Rights are incomplete without women's rights. Even before forgetting one brutal incident of Dr Priyanka another took place. Let this be an opportunity for all of us to renew our pledge of zero tolerance toward gender-based violence and unflinching support for the advancement of women's rights. Gender Justice is a must for sustainable development. Besides, a harsh decision on capital punishment is inevitable. Think of it!!"

◈

"Effective communication through moral education alone is the mot juste to prevent many heinous crimes!"

◈

"While sitting in opposition every legislative becomes Ersatz Saint and sermonises the ruling government!

◈

"Learn to teach and teach to learn!"

◆

"The advent of nuclear weapons was intended to make the military more powerful than ever. Nonetheless, unerringly the opposite happened - confronted with devices that could factually blow the world into pieces!

◆

"The coup de grâce for the justice in any of the brutal crimes should be a lesson to all evil forces! "

◆

"In my opinion, an individual or a nation that cannot win a war should not give a sermon about peace!"

◆

"The oxymoron state of Indian politics is rather very typical! The political groups or individuals that oppose something would support the same thing as soon as they change their group!!"

◆

"Most Indians got triskaidekaphobia. Astoundingly, thirteen is my lucky number! "

◆

"A pauper if becomes wealthy would often be pursy and haughty. But the born rich are often meek! "

◆

"Bygone are the days when uneducated people remained delightfully tractable. But education and cultural learning, in conjunction with effective communication, has changed the entire scenario! "

◆

"I don't understand why every impugning activity in India is ultimately interrelated to the caste and creed of the affected person! "

"Whenever I read a good old book, I feel that the vanished delectation and reflex for the glory of the author is still pertinent through that work. I believe my books also would give such a feeling to my future readers! "

"A spider weaves the web to catch insects. However, sometimes it gets trapped on the web. Political webs weaved by great leaders often yield the same results! "

"The petulant and fussy leaders are ever ready to instigate the feelings of their followers - often bestowed with personal interests! "

"I guess the word 'aught' is derived from the word 'athi' used by Biharis!"

"They refer to the Internet as the eighth wonder. But for me, it is the only wonder! "

"In India, the true minorities are the taxpayers. Is it not so?!!??"

"Due to my experience, I have comprehended that there's always someone who is ever ready to play a flibbertigibbet in every conversation. "

"From sometime before, India has been whipsawed by increasing crime rates and plunging employment, whereas it should be the time to grow steadily safer and more prosperous after the nation has become technologically advanced! "

"It is clear that most of the political decisions cannot be revoked for the reason that they are impervious to any sort of external pressure. Then why damage the public property that would ultimately burden the entire people of the nation?! "

"The clarion call that everyone should give to their intuition, on the new year day, is to be the best human - a person with morals and ethics! "

"Do new year celebrations mean the shindig and parties in pubs? This is what is happening in the adopted Indian culture! "

"Once I retire from my job, it's my wish to spend some time gallivanting all over the world to understand different cultures and people ... to pen my travelogues! "

"I wonder if there exists any person without even a minor foible! "

"I often find people start protesting on the streets without knowing segregating exaggerations and mendacious claims from the veracity of facts! "

"We should support protests that do not cause damage to the public property. What do we meet by damaging public property? Everything has to come from within - let it be owning the public property as ours or practising Swatchch Bharat! "

"Those born in 1970's and 1980's- the period of belle epoque- have seen the actual technological evolution. I am fortunate for being one of those lucky people! "

"To me, it is giving the feel of gulf war redux due to the spell of unseasonably raising prices of fuel! "

"One season's skyrocketing prices of one or other commodities in India lead to a surfeit of excess production of the same in the next season - ultimately resulting in the hike of other commodities! "

"The Idea of changing the mind of an adamant is just like the efforts put in by our predecessors to convert the base metals into gold, using the Elixir by the practice of alchemy!"

"Whenever I see books in my library, I sense a feeling that they are offering up the vanished past for our delectation and reflex nostalgia. "

"With the advent of technology, the lives have become mechanical...they just appeal weal but wretched! "

"Human error is the main expanse upon which social engineering relies!"

◆

"A lily-livered warrior or a politician can never be successful! "

◆

"I don't find any difference between a few crooked people and werewolves -- except for the hirsute appearance of the latter!"

◆

"I wanna live my youthful years vicariously through my kids by filling up their lives with so much fun that I have missed out! "

◆

"In making decisions, often people glom on to other's ideas instead of caring for their conscience! "

◆

"Both peace and war demand dauntless persistence to achieve the very objective - minimal damage and no casualties! "

◆

"In inorder to meet the success, bonhomie among teammates is as significant as the team spirit! "

◆

"In the contemporary society, certainly, the more coruscate you are, the more successful you will be! "

◆

"Almost every NRI is trying to own the Western Culture. In this process, they consider their native heritage and culture as an outlandish entity! "

◆

"It may sometimes happen that few seemingly waste and antique pieces discovered in a frowsy ancestral home could turn out to be very valuable! "

"The pulse of voters can never be predicted! despite a great struggle, some of the well-deserving candidates lose due to a lacklustre voting percentage!! "

"Just like the ice crystals melt within no time as the air turns warmer, the patriotism in people sublimates away as the date in the calendar changes! "

"From the time when the boom of lands surrounded by cities started gaining the market value, many became rich, overnight! However, many people denigrated it as mere parvenu!!"

"It amounts to a galling defeat if someone fails to succeed even after a diligent effort! "

"Until and unless both sides of an argument agree to an armistice, there won't be any further action that could lead towards an amicable solution! "

◆

"A very few people are born with a purpose and lead their attainments for an amaranthine existence! "

◆

"I strongly believe that due to the presence of alternate banking channels, the bank strikes are having a stifling effect. No doubt that

this is an untold and macabre fact for the reason that strikes are proven ineffectual, despite the best efforts put in by all the beholders!"

"The idea of establishing the Indian Institute of Heritage is a good initiative to reinstate the heritage and culture, which fell into desuetude after India has undergone cultural imperialism for a few centuries! "

"The inclined level of the offering of freebies to the masses has successfully prognosticated the outcomes of the Indian elections, well in advance!"

"Most people think peace is the absence of a conflict. But it is beyond that! "

"A knowledgeable person can use his ideas either in a scumbled or glazed way! "

"Social Media has been facilitating political parties to indulge in political indoctrination - persuading people to believe what the political parties exactly want! "

"Terrorism is an extreme form of communication - often resulting due to brainwashing! "

"To overcome the media coverage, which is proven stronger than the will of the government, the latter for a very long time has used the exciting punctuation! "

"It is indubitably correct that the power of making war often prevents it. Thus, effective communication should be able to prevent war!"

"In India, as evidenced in the Nirbhaya case, it takes more time before the execution of capital punishment for the reason that it takes more levels of verification and consumption of time before the mercy petition of the defendant would be expunged by the honourable president!"

"The print media by its obvious nature is primarily exoteric. Yet it has always had an esoteric side for the reason that it is meant for literates!"

"The social media has turned into such a stupid platform that right from players to politicians everyone is quickly going back to the dugout as insults and obloquy rains down from the netizens, as soon as the expectations of people go down!"

"Success needs a special attitude in a person - not to resile from one's ambitions!"

"The occasional gustatory pleasure of Bara Khana (feast) in Armed Forces' messes is the nostalgic recollection to almost every defence veteran!"

"Political coalition should be based on the sterling and intrinsic merit of the constituents rather than the adscititious or ephemeral benefits! "

"The once neglected and dilapidated fields located in the outskirts of a city have now taken the shape of costly villas and apartments! "

CHAPTER TWO

Musings 2

"Be the philanthropist -- there's an acute shortage of this category of people in this world dominated by the disparagers! "

"If a soft-hearted person turns into a cold-hearted, the culmination would be insufferable! "

"The world without humans will be the best place for other creatures on the earth! "

"We do not have control over worst situations but can have reign over worst people!"

"If life is a journey, we don't have sway over the beginning but the end could be contrived! "

"An organisation loses the power over some of its employees when the latter don't expect anything from the organisation -- including the promotions! "

"If a person does not have control over accomplishment, he can not be conceded as a leader!"

◈

"Donors should impose a self-limit, for no receiver can have such a limit! If not followed, within a short time there would be a role reversal!!"

◈

"Being genuine to everyone and everything could be a great punishment!"

◈

"Some writers think that it's better to confuse if not able to convince -- resurfaced in their writings as rigmarole!"

◈

"The little information that an individual or nation could glean about the enemy would benefit in the adversary planning!"

◈

"The blind mind cannot behold the beauty!"

◈

"Human life is a pendulum that oscillates between the regression and progression -- can't keep the same place constantly!"

◈

"In life, problems are always associated with cry outs. But unfortunately, we don't consider those vociferations seriously!"

◈

"Behind every change, there is a proportionate learning; and behind every learning, there is a corresponding suffering!"

◆

"Simplification of rules should be undertaken for efficacy, for it is obvious that people would be vexed to go through the rigmarole of ways! "

◆

"To be a successful spy, you need to have the ability to glean! "

◆

"Proper reflections cannot be possible through a shaking mirror or turbulent waters -- the mind is a similar entity! "

◆

"The soldiers and farmers do informally swear fealty to the nation and the palpable relation between this fraternity and the nation is implied in their oath of fealty! "

◆

"Time elapses unnoticed in the jocund company of good books! "

◆

"Unfortunately, most people are ever ready to lead their ears to calumny! "

◆

"Every political party is harried with badgering the opponents until the matter becomes a point of debate in the media! "

◆

"If you can make someone contemplate about something, it coequals teaching a valuable lesson!"

◆

"Out of passion, people do anything that satisfies their self. However, the same passion, at times, torments them to the end! "

◈

"Predisposition is the best weapon that a dunce can have! "

◈

"Before being there for others, one should not leave him behind! "

◈

"It is easier being the judge than a participant! "

◈

"Truth is a single shot vaccine while a lie is a multi-dosage!"

◈

"The relationship between true education and personality development is intrinsic! "

◈

"Politicians have their way of inveigling into whatever can be inveigled! "

◈

"There's a dire need for states to forswear obtention of nuclear weapons and promote peace among its stakeholders! "

◈

"Peace is the apotheosis of spunk! "

◈

"Animus loses its prominence if every problem becomes a tussle!"

◈

"The only similarity between affluent and nomadic groups is the spatial mobility -- of course, the purposes are entirely different!"

"The more a person acquires philosophical knowledge, the more will be his acquired thesaurus! "

"Parenting is the same across all walks of life -- the only difference is some are expressive and some aren't! "

"Middle ground might make a good parasol but a craptastic dome! "

"It's not necessary that angelic faces have angelic souls! "

"Some incidents in life desiccate the goodness in a person -- turning the virtues into obelisk!"

"You may have your reasons and I have my validations! "

"Today's corrupted leaders are tomorrow's whilom great!"

"Not every problem could be resolved by reordering buffers and scheduling algorithms! "

"If the associates are such, even the wise could be transformed into a repugnant oaf!"

◆

"If freebies are extended to those who are hale and hearty, the debacle of the nation is not far along! "

◆

"The exquisite workmanship could be intuited only through the bijou system! "

◆

"The appreciation of gormandizing comes only from a famished person! "

◆

"The speech becomes meaningful only if its value addition is more than silence! "

◆

"There's no wonder that humans may learn principles of humanity from animals tamed by themselves! "

◆

"Your journey towards wisdom begins when your knowledge admits that you hardly know anything! "

◆

"Irrespective of the physical appearance of a person, every kind heart is innately resplendent! "

◆

"The quondam academic curriculum of ancient India was much more exotic than the one adopted at present! "

◆

"The problem with many is they consider feelings and emotions is the same! "

◈

"Ideas emerge out from the mind, only when its faucet is open! "

◈

"The unethical corporations are managing to mulct lakhs of rupees from innocent and poor people! "

◈

"Life is a continuous process of aleatory situations wherein time plays the role of throwing of dice! "

◈

"The prodigy oftentimes cast by an evil eye! "

◈

"The life's bitter truth is that we comprehend the worth of a person or a thing either before possession or after losing that! "

◈

"Cataracts, the steep rapids in a river, represent our ephemeral emotions! "

◈

"To carry on both plussed and nonplussed at the same time is, of course, a rarity of its kind! "

◈

"Retrospective view of one's past can pave a Kingsway for one's future! "

◈

"Both freedom and respect are not given -- they are rather earned!!"

◈

"There is a hidden scientific reason behind the traditional shibboleths of Hindu Religious rituals! "

◈

"One of the reasons behind our anger is the involvement in floundering around trying to understand unnecessary things! "

◈

"In this world wherein even a person with minimal knowledge also pretends as if the omniscient, there are some greater and meek personalities that admit hardly they know anything! "

◈

"Mostly, people would not comprehend circumstances totally until and unless they meet a similar situation! "

◈

"The dynamics of politics could be changed while the nation could pick up the locale of a developed country, only if educated electorates get rid of political torpor! "

◈

"Let it be an artist or an author, they leave behind to posterity a titanic bevvy of the paragon that would stay eternal! "

◈

"When there's no means of encountering the threat of occasionalism in real-time situations, it can be just parried with silence, the best way of communicating! "

◈

"We seldom realise that most of the Daedalian problems have duck soup solutions!"

"One should have been hitherto suffered immensely to become full of oneself! "

"Excessive corporate fundings herald criminalization of political punters! "

"Wonders transpire if professionalism is infused with gusto!"

"No one owes anything to anyone for their self-driven action that has no direct or indirect effect on the latter!"

"No one and nothing can purloin the knowledge gained by a person! "

"Movements of life are very dynamic that when someone is on a down the up cannot be far away! "

"It is the precedence and priorities that put the other issues firmly back into next place among the immediate concerns!"

"When a satisfactory answer cannot be grounded-in, politicians astutely parry the questions posed by the media people! "

"The palpable biased reporting that takes sides of an issue by some media channels has been mirroring the capricious world of media and its greedy business conglomerates! "

◈

"One of the barriers to effectual business communication is the inarticulate guttural grunt by the members of an organisation -- both in vertical and horizontal channels!"

◈

"Managements have become so crazy that they irrationally expect its employees to do the tango among the teacups! "

◈

"Most of the societies have still not developed into such a noble status to comprehend the plutonic relationship between a boy and girl! "

◈

"Grounded vehemence will lead to serenity -- retention of one's sangfroid!"

◈

"To appreciate the glimmer, one should have been into the tenebrosity of murk! "

◈

"States have set the seal on promoting the English language by designing the courses to emphasize lexical skills among the students while ignoring the furtherance of native languages!"

◈

"If reporting is all about objectivity then the process can be appreciated as a domino effect!"

"The memoirs of a soldier could veer into hagiography only if the soldier is given carte blanche to express his views!"

"Without getting any chance, how can someone prove his mettle?! "

"The difference between classroom and life is -- in classroom learning comes first and exam thereupon while in life exam comes first and learning afterwards! "

"Even the empathetic and bounteous hearts savvy exasperation and pique! "

"I often find the primetime news debates as a scathing jeremiad against the meaningless invasions of privacy!"

"When there's no best choice among the probable options, what we choose will be a mere bivouac that makes a good umbrella but a poor roof!"

"Although business meetings are intended for value addition, oftentimes the entire schedule is spent with palaver about useless discussions!"

"Don't tolerate rather terminate a problem!"

"Non-verbal communication is all about communicating what could not be said and making the receiver hear that part as well! "

"A good diarize should answer all whys and wherefores!"

"If you have a purpose in the life, you won't have the leisure to dally about! "

"To have the panoramic view, one needs to reach the apex! "

"It insinuates that you have mastered the art of acting if you can amuse everyone!"

"For each magnum opus, there are corresponding several pinchbeck replicas! "

"It takes no time to turn the irresistible pulchritude into grotesqueness -- unlike benignity that builds on perpetual inner beauty! "

CHAPTER THREE

Musings 3

"Artistry is the purpose, lead and outcome of any war!"

"Often people have so much compassion for others while forgetting to give it a share to oneself!"

"A perfect research design should transmogrify a pilot study into an exemplary post-intervention evaluation!"

"When one feels something as his responsibility, he takes the pain of bearing the weight; but when it becomes a burden, he dribbles the heaviness!"

"Either one has to berate or tolerate to react against worsened unsolicited matters!"

"Moral obligation is a definite prerogative that also concerns reacting aptly against what is not fair, not right and not just! "

"A man never becomes sagacious merely by serendipity -- it's the result of a well-thought concoction!"

"It's better to expel the darkness surrounded by one's shack rather than lit a light in another's shant!"

"Instead of taking a flexuous path, the last leg career path should be straight enough to lead the rest of the life smoothly -- a well chalked out plan is a must for the same!"

"The richest legacy that needs to be passed on to generations is all about heritage, ethics and moral values! "

"People who mortgage their individuality or greatest souls alone can hope to be liked by everyone!"

"All art forms call for the Meraki in the performer, to give the alchemical bliss to the audience!"

"One should know the precedence and associativity of operators, before tending to infix, to convey the exact and intended meaning!"

"The contemporary situation of ethics of any profession is merely a moot concept! "

"Maybe respect is the befitting substitute for the platonic love! "

◆

"If you find there's a dissimilitude in the information that you receive from more than two sources then that information is not true -- merely a bumf!"

◆

"Ignorance is far better than the pseudo enlightenment!"

◆

"The greatest strengths of an individual are determination and resilience!"

◆

"The companionship of good books can turn an abject man into an intractable man!"

◆

"The brilliance in a person awakens in perplexity! "

◆

"I usually don't go astray because I am forthright -- not learnt to be insincere!"

◆

"In this world of insalubrious feuding competition, one has to blow his own trumpet if wants to stay intact in the race!"

◆

"Good or bad, emotions need to be given an immediate voice; else, they will come in front at unsolicited times, for emotions do not pass away!"

◆

"The bewitchment of a person's intelligence lies in his communication abilities -- both the spoken and unspoken!"

◈

"In the society of backstabbing and obnoxious people, even the clever should act sometimes as helpless nimrods! "

◈

"There is a vast difference between being orthodox and being culturally conditioned!"

◈

"You can judge me as genuine when I do vociferate and strike a balance when I just stay unresponsive!"

◈

"The abundance of something at one place equals the insufficiency of the same thing at other places!"

◈

"The callow sportspersons if given proper training, shall bring incredible laurels to the nation!"

◈

"Wisdom and experience go hand in hand! "

◈

"Practicing ethics and morals meticulously can also cause moral and philosophical conundrum!"

◈

"Sagacity becomes void in doing something that doesn't harm anyone while giving contentment to an individual! "

◈

"There's no wonder that my books make me have a well deserved to kvell over -- after all I have worked so hard on those projects!"

"Till the time a person cannot realise that it is the achievement of goals that make a person beatific and not people, he keeps on foraging happiness! "

"When the ship sinks in the middle of the ocean, it makes no difference whether one knows swimming or not! "

"Nothing can travel faster than a scuttlebutt! "

"The more the agony you have experienced, the more commiserate you are!"

"The choice of using one's knowledge can either be for self progression or for another's retrogression!"

"You are the only person who can give the best answer to your muddle!"

"Just like charity, patriotism should also begin at home!"

"It's obvious that human emotions are undulant just like our thought process!"

"We need a particular countenance to show enmity or express love -- in its dearth slowly the relevant thoughts get wiped out!"

"A single instance is enough to form an opinion -- favouring or opposing, but needs a constant effort to keep up the things as they are!"

"Time and again it has been proven that it's a bromide that truth alone prevails!"

"I oftentimes realise slender youth with tousled hair have a great quality -- don't live either in the past or future but only in the present!"

"The corporate world is never be generous -- simply serve the pink slips to defenestrate the employees overnight!"

"The most important thing that I have learnt in my life is - to be stronger alone!"

"A lot of pain and risk is associated with bringing together the like herding cats!"

"It's not about getting the hang of skills of using weapons that make a great warrior but knowing to use the right weapon at the right time!"

"In this world of fake people, It's important to winnow, down to earth people from unrealistic people!"

"Even to the wisest of wise, it becomes very difficult to understand the political sophistry!"

"We need to stay aghast at the idiosyncrasies while honouring the native heritage and culture, at the same time!"

"The Guided Missile: Memoirs of an Air Warrior is a book that would ever remain the beginning -- everything is introductory, liminal and prefatory!"

◆

"Turning a blind eye is an art, mastering which proves a person as a casuist!"

◆

"They say when in anger we should refrain from both action and speech, but by doing so we are forgetting that we are grounding the true feelings by compromising!"

◆

"My virtues are my strongest enemies!"

◆

"Never take everything for granted -- even the strongest feelings do have peripheral limits!"

◆

"Most cryptic comments are sarcastic, but some are true!"

◆

"It's the lion that needs to be ennobled and not the nimrod if the story belongs to the latter!"

◆

"All those who can't execute their ideas are mere slaves!"

◆

"If a decision made cannot be ossified, there is no meaning it to be considered as a strong decision!"

◆

"Like a fugitive, bookaholics rarely leave their secluded cabin!"

◆

"A soldier's hubris is what makes him unique among his civilian counterparts when he turns into a veteran!"

◆

"Watering the obnoxious weeds would yield no fruits!"

◆

"To me, nothing is more despicable than claiming the credit of others as one's own!"

◆

"Give a proper shape to your considerations, if you don't want yourself a bondslave!"

◆

"Winning is easy to the enemy if treachery is within us!"

◆

"Our understanding of philosophy lies in learning about the beauty of austerity and renunciation!"

"The scum of the society is taking the form of parasites that seek undue freebies!"

"The society takes a trip down memory lane of only those who are uplifted and not those who are behind one's orotund!"

"Many organisations fail to realise that extortion of extended working hours yields no positive results, for employees simply spend time lollygagging around!"

"The most prodigious rectitude is seared with scars!"

"The art of volition includes looking the other way also!"

"Yes, it is my strongest numinous feeling that God prevails through the soldiers and farmers!"

""Of course, philosophical thoughts are patently absurd!""
- Monday, 30 August, 2021, 7:37:40 PM

"The forte of a leader is seen in the acolyte!"

"History does never transmogrify from comfort zones!"

"My silence is my gangsta!"

"Most people confound tenderness with frailty!"

"The desultory and undisciplined voters don't deserve a right to question the government!"

"Certain regnant beliefs do not allow us to go against the preconceived ideologies!"

"Certainly, on this moving wheel of life, everyone will be doffed their past and repent at some or other time for their untoward deeds!"

"The wisest decision is to stay mute amidst fools though you have to say so much!"

"The most successful people master the art of Gasconade!"

"Hold your head high so that the shadow falls behind!"

"Behind every bad story of a person that you are exposed to, there's a good story that we need to know! "

"Predicaments make us ill at ease!"

"Anxiety can stop a person in his tracks and hold him back. It is easier said than practising to face the fears and push through them. Yet, it is very essential to get through!"

"With conviction, people could indeed make plans but whether they would be effective or not depends on the Almighty!"

"Having a child leave home after taking a job would be looked upon as a measure of success — an insignia that parents had prepared them for society. Nonetheless, the downsides are customarily not agreeably accredited!"

"Without a doubt, even in this era of reasoning complemented by logical deductions, at times, we are forced to accept certain things as true!"

"Yes, there is no doubt that when we listen to music, it triggers parts of the brain that bring to mind certain emotions associated with specific memories!"

"To the best of my contemplations, there would be no convinced time when late-night turns into the early morning — it would be, on the whole, a matter of mere stance!"

"Changing the coiffure is probably the first blow every soldier faces in his professional life!"

"To escape oneself, people suborn others into the machination!"

"It amounts to an egregious breach of humanly respect and etiquette to not offer due to veneration to the one who helped you in need!"

"It's only the bold media that can fulminate against the untoward issues in the society!"

"At times, the silence becomes a dire need among many things!"

"If life is to be considered as a game, people try to win over mostly by sledging!"

"Without undertaking trials and tribulations, extraordinary results are impossible!"

CHAPTER FOUR

Musings 4

"If the ship sinks in the middle of the sea, being a master or ignorant of swimming would hardly make any difference!"

"A true leader can lead even without a title -- a status otherwise is a mere decoration!"

"One of the strange observations I ever had is, the person who has never worn the shoe also teaches you the way to tie laces!"

"You are groomed well, only if you treat a janitor and the chief alike!"

"Mostly, an egghead's room is found with the books that have stacked high in precarious towers!"

"Any biopic could be seen as a series of vignettes showing the lives of celebrities!"

"Usually, people of the same ilk become close to each other; and collude with one another!"

◆

"Explanations do not carry any value when already someone's actions have revealed the true intentions!"

◆

"Even exhaustion has become an element of a status symbol in this contemporary competitive world!"

◆

"I have never been paranoid, for my instinct always gives the exact vibes!"

◆

"For each changing day, I am a different man in some or other way!"

◆

"Behind every tender-hearted person, there's a definite compassionate story!"

◆

"It's the passion that brings perfection to the work!"

◆

"The world can be shaken even in a reposeful way -- the gentle way of contemplation!"

◆

"Every attempt to take revenge paves a way to two graves!"

◆

"The skill of a great author could be sensed through his talent of shaping inchoate vignettes into a masterpiece!"

◆

"If parents and teachers are not allowed to chastise, how could we expect a child to learn the best?!"

◆

"It's a million-dollar question, why the policy documents of almost every organisation are always formulated using the obtuse language!"

◆

"In the process of not letting down others, one should not get himself let down!"

◆

"A family to cater for is much more important than the community to overawe!"

◆

"When I find a so neatly maintained secondhand book, the only question that bothers me is -- has the book been truly read by someone or not?"

◆

"War is a game of right and left -- who is right and what is left!"

◆

"If it is not serene, it's not effective leadership!"

◆

"Oftentimes, the approval of something by an acclaimed leading light is what parlay that entity!"

◆

"The filial responsibility is an eternal responsibility!"

◈

"An individual that remains intransigent in his efforts, in the long run, would grab the success!"

◈

"Oftentimes, the competent authorities show the cavalier attitude about spending public money -- quadrant four priorities are treated as quadrant one priorities!"

◈

"The scions of business tycoons can only find plenty of readily available options -- rest all have to compromise in some or other way!"

◈

"It is the instinct that parents get fretted over every detail of their offsprings' performance!"

◈

"Compromising means lowering one's standards to accommodate those who refuse to raise their standards!"

◈

"Incidentally, there's a win in some of the losses!"

◈

"Everything concerning a conflict is equally odious to me, for conflicts are inhuman!"

◈

"Almost every organisation has a cabal that works against the sincere and loyal employees, for they feel a hidden threat!"

◈

"If the stories are not embellished, they won't entice much of the reader's interest!"

"The fine line between confidence and overconfidence is like gossamer!"

"Never sell your best weapon to someone just for the reason you love him!"

"If the choice is to be made between harsh honesty and dulcet falsity, one should prefer the former to later!"

"In this false-hearted world of people, an individual is given respect according to one's social status!"

"Neither every meliorist is a libtard nor every libtard is a meliorist!"

"A person could be judged perfectly by the way he treats the janitor -- not by the way he behaves with the highest authority!"

"Soliloquies are one of the best forms of intrapersonal communication!"

"An artistic work itself is a world that reflects the emotions of the artist!"

"Tenacity alone is not enough to win a conflict -- a proper strategy and its execution are much weighty in the context!"

◆

"Life is Just like a mirage that we chase at every instance and is hovered before our eyes!"

◆

"Both the process of learning and unlearning is equally significant to live the purest form of life, just like a child!"

◆

"Only a few people master the art of personality development, which doesn't consider either the success or failure!"

◆

"If we meticulously follow an autobiography, we can live the life of the person described therein!"

◆

"Some people think much about the society and ween of themselves in other's viewpoint -- simply forget the very fact that people don't have time even for their problems!"

◆

"Having no formal gatekeepers, social media has turned to be a platform for the audience to hector the wonky!"

◆

"One can discern the generation gap very easily, if something becomes hard-won for you, while the next generation feels it is facile!"

◆

"The success of a story, whether it be of a movie or a book, depends greatly on the narrative style of involving treacle!"

◆

"I am fond of my mirror, for it always presents the best person who can change my life as desired when I am in front of it!"

◆

"To me, dithering and procrastination have always been intransitive!"

◆

"The desultory life and the rudderless ship will lead nowhere!"

◆

"Conflicts are the outcome of communication failure!"

◆

"It's true that happiness lies in simplicity. But simplicity has difficulty as its base!"

◆

"Logically, war should happen only when peace creates a problem!"

◆

"The same stone could either turn into a stumbling block or a stepping stone!"

◆

"There's a thin line between shamelessly buttering up and hobnobbing!"

◆

"A few autobiographical narrations and contemplations make us live the character role of biographer!"

◆

"Any number of postulation could see through the light when the veracity finds its strongest roots!"

◆

"There's always an associated resistance to adopting new technologies -- the first phase is meant for the peers' approval!"

◆

"Understanding and breaking the obsolete strategies is the fundamental point in comprehending the art of war!"

◆

"Time is the foremost governing reason for the efficacy of everything -- what was the best before aeons could turn into an obsolete one after a period!"

◆

"There's no wrong if an individual is different from others, provided there's no harm to his associates and the society!"

◆

"Let it be good or bad, what becomes significant is not the act but the intention behind that act!"

◆

"How inspiring an individual may be, at last, he too would have to become a cadaver one day!"

◆

"Failure is nothing but a mere wrongly proven decision!"

◆

"Luck is a game-changer -- no one knows what impact it will have on the people!"

◈

"There's a difference between celebrating the achievements after one's birth, and celebrating one's birth itself -- I have regard only for the former!"

◈

"In a larger context, many significant issues would turn out to be trivial!"

◈

"Amidst many viewpoints and many priorities, each and everything has its significance!"

◈

"One thing the entire humankind forgets is that irrespective of any sort of differences, all are mere humans!"

◈

"People are pre-programmed in accordance to the societal and religious codes!"

◈

"Film is a wonderful mass media -- when the emotions plotted in the film are at resonance with the emotions of the audience, the audience experiences an enthralling feeling!"

◈

"Without content, style alone won't work -- whether it be a book or movie!"

◈

"Fear has no form -- it's a mere fallacy!"

◈

"If the reason could be analysed, fear can be diminished to a greater extent!"

◆

"Imagination and fear are intermingled!"

◆

"It's impossible to comprehend how an idea takes the birth just like a lightning!"

◆

"It is the perception about a thing or person that makes an ordinary thing exceptional!"

◆

"One should be the master of his ideas but not ideas should become his master!"

◆

"If goat makes friendship with the grass, what does it eat?"

◆

"There's something good that can be taken even from the most useless creäture!"

◆

"Life is the comedy show that is visualised in the tragic form!"

◆

"Music strongly works on the mental status of the humans!"

◆

"The bitter truth is -- most people want to see the debacle of the others, despite the fact they pretend to enjoy the success!"

"In this world of fallacies, only a few people master the art of living their lives king-size!"

"I always want to explore what happens to me when I am in deep sleep!"

"It's a waste to spend even a second time on the job that you don't like while it's worth spending many hours on the job you are most interested in!"

"I never force anyone to live my life nor would like to live theirs. However, if I strongly don't like something in a person, I just move away!"

"Deep discussions with good people will enhance our knowledge portfolio to a greater extent!"

"Revenge is both good and bad -- only circumstances decide if it is good or bad!"

"This world is full of Satya Harishchandras who don't stand by their own words!"

"If our personality has to change at every instant in life, individuality means nothing of its kind!"

"According to me, a complete man is as complex as an ocean -- so far didn't find any such single inspiring personality!"

"In the laboratory called society, I ever remain a researcher!"

"I do observe each and everything so meticulously. But would never let others know about my observations, until and unless the situation warrants the same!"

"I admire how something is being presented and not what is being presented -- that's why I love screenplay and narrative style, the most!"

"Change is inevitable -- what appears novel at the moment becomes obsolete at the next moment!"

CHAPTER FIVE

Musings 5

"In the modern electronic warfare, absolutely no scope exists for subterfuge and concealment. Nonetheless, modern warfare guarantees turning swords into ploughshares!"

"Exquisite sense of timing is one of the significant characteristics that every artist should have!"

"The still-simmering offers of freebies in India would lead to unconscionable welshing and ruin the nation-state and thereby continue to foment precariousness!"

"The biographies of some leading lights happen with the stipulation of verbiage -- because -- biographers recognise that the reader would lose the flavour, even if a single word misses out!"

"One of the great qualities of some famous people is that they never purport to be a kind of oracle in the métier they master!"

"It is the fiduciary primary responsibility of the parents to ensure successful build-out of traits and etiquettes among the children -- the

future of the universe!"

◆

"The Sisyphean task of finding a way to get people to the warranted positions remains unchanged until and unless the selection rules are made transparent and happen only based on pure merit!"

◆

"Official cronyism and high level of malversations are the few constituents of civilization that disengage evolution!"

◆

"If jaundiced eyes denote looking upon something with prejudice, limpid eyes denote benignant expression!"

◆

"Those, who delve into every activity with ardour, would be contemplated as an asset to the establishment!"

◆

"One of the finest obiter dicta is -- the fountainhead of the melody of Illaiyaraja's music has a stranglehold that spells magical sanative!"

◆

"It's not a big deal to practice work-life balance while you rise to the bait to stay a bit too ubiquitous at work!"

◆

"Some people who keep up rapacious relations could productively poison the ears -- even prove a gentleman as an impostor and the one that swindles as the innocent!"

◆

"Even after a lot of efforts, sometimes the whole ball of vax connected with the processes of a lengthy and operose herculean task

goes in vain!"

◆

"Peace is a notion of shared amity and congruence in the absence of resentment and ferocity — an absence of skirmish. In a broader sense, peace is freedom from fear of violence flanked by individuals or groups!"

◆

"Agrarian society is the only section in the world that receives bubkes for its high-priced exertion!"

◆

"Even at times, the sky turns into a pale translucent blue. But never came across any translucent grimace in the voice of SP Balasubramaniam -- it was luculent always, without any exception!"

◆

"Ingenious leaders are uncommon -- at once they become emollient, self-critical and articulate, in a way that put initially bashful followers at their ease!"

◆

"It needs an unfeigned entrance of a third party to arrive at an amicable solution to an acrimonious fight between two persons or nations!"

◆

"Never give up attitude and a rambunctious routine of unabated practice towards magnificence is the secret of success of many efficient people!"

◆

"Usually the division among members of one group spares few members to abstain from decision-making -- the same becomes helpful

to the other groups in attaining unanimity!"

◆

"It is palpable that social media has thrown down the gauntlet to mainstream media by giving the best -- what the media consumers want in the real-time!"

◆

"It is the basic instinct that teaches a bird to carefully make a sinuous nest out of twigs. Similarly, humans too have some instincts -- influenced by many external forces!"

◆

"It's not always necessary to restrain oneself with a bevvy of restrictions just to behave with a bit of savoir-faire!"

◆

"It makes no sense to convince a pachyderm -- because -- such people act according to their own will and wish -- have no concern for approved ethos!"

◆

"I am neither a pessimist nor an optimist -- I am just a meliorist for I strongly believe that every positive action is in some or other way related to another positive action happening in the world!"

◆

"It's a great wonder to folks of this generation that how could our forebears survive in the world without the Internet, the eighth wonder of the world!"

◆

"Proper planning and execution are the rudimentary needs for professional and pecuniary plans to go along with successful accomplishment!"

"Some men are born to greatness. Others carve their part in it -- a few who make the nation proud!"

"Many charity trusts, over a time, usually pretermit the very purpose -- probably the premeditation of succeeding trustees doesn't sync with the founders; besides, they embezzle a lot!"

"The leitmotif for the actions undertaken by many trade unions may be greater divergence in pay -- one of the inescapable megatrends!"

"Public relations behest employment of someone who shills to simply extol the wonders of the organisation through effective communication!"

"The pertinacious ingenuity is a two-edged personality trait that may not yield the desired result invariably!"

"An individual's mythomania would ultimately drag him into the ditch!"

◈

"Due to the social media usurp, the mainstream media is not able to take up its place of conversation as intended!"

◈

"The benefic inevitability of sustainable development could be better realised by analysing worst affected natural calamities!"

◈

"Trying to please an intransigent fool is not worthy ... for it would ultimately turn out a futile attempt!"

◈

"No government ever succeeded welshing on their election promises. More so, the belief is that freebies given to the parasite electorates would bring them back into power!"

◈

"There is enough evidence that most clinical trials on variegated vaccines being developed have demonstrated insufficient immunogenicity!"

◈

"There is an urgent need of desegregating significant policies that are still in force from the period of colonial rule -- to revive for the contemporary needs!"

◈

"Genuine friends know the obverse and reverse side of each other -- if not, it cannot be considered true companionship!"

◈

"The quotidian experiences at the workplace have given me an understanding of the pragmatic approach to business communication!"

◈

"A blooming visage may not always be the index of the happy heart -- sometimes there's a hidden melancholy behind it!"

◈

"To protect oneself from backstabbing, everyone needs to have a virtual dorsal shell, like a turtle has an actual one!"

"There's no wonder that even a well-established entrepreneur would tend to be on the bearish side at times!"

"There's a hidden talent in most of the guttersnipe. All that we lack is adroitness to dig out that knack in them!"

"Sophomoric sense of humour is thy name of immatureness!"

"These days banking activities have become truculent demeanour -- make every banker unpleasant to work with!"

"The decisions taken unilaterally without the consent of other stakeholders would have to be rued at some point in time!"

"Many people do not know that applauding between concerts of classical music amounts to disrespect for it amounts to opprobrium for the composer's and performer's scheme!"

"It is not always necessary that soldiers exult in the kill and keep mementoes of their victims!"

"Most people would realise, all together, in their terminal phase of life that they were poor and dependent even though basking in the jollity of wealth!"

"Nowadays the corporate termination policies are so harsh that sensitive people won't even swat off a fly in a similar way!"

◆

"A very long time in writing, some books turn into jaw-dropping masterpieces, with one bravura concatenation of narration topping the one before!"

◆

"Parents are their children's greatest inspiration -- they build, create and nurture -- they are children's greatest sources!"

◆

"Having a lovely father is like getting a treasure pack, filled with a lot of captivating surprises!"

◆

"A father is like a mirror for every child -- fathers reflect around their children in every step they take. Besides, they are more like warriors that fight every battle their children might want to face!"

◆

"A leader by its meaning goes first and leads by example so that others are motivated to follow him/her!"

◆

"It is a general observation that most of the time we know about the people who are in positions of leadership but not endowed with leadership. So, it is understood that a position of office is no guarantee of leadership!"

◆

"To be a leader a person must have an innate commitment to the goal that he will strive to achieve even if nobody follows him!"

◈

"Expelling the multifarious attitudes from oneself is the only way to get rid of many pains that we experience every day!"

◈

"Social Media participation has become a part of everyone's daily schedule -- it's no longer the bailiwick of geeks!"

◈

"Though one knows that his ideal is very far away and there will be a lot of difficulties to face, he should never give up -- must complete that ideal and should not abnegate! "

◈

"Similar to the way a farrier meticulously puts shoes on racehorses and takes part in its overall success, a counsellor contributes phenomenally to meet success for his trainee!"

◈

"These days, people with morals and ethical standards are found in infinitesimal quantities among large sediments of dregs!"

◈

"To be a rationalist is not necessarily to be a libertine as argued by a few!"

◈

"Some people do never gain ground in their lives for they do always snivel about their despondent past than thinking about sanguine future!"

◈

"The fulvous fallen faded leaves remind us of the terminal phase of our lives -- no longer joined by the originally possessed!"

"Freebies given relentlessly to the undeserving people, out of the taxpayers' money, just for the sake of grabbing a few more votes in elections has long been a bugbear for many!"

"Before some suggestions become strongest actions, they needed to be turned into one cohesive proposal beforehand!"

"What would be the fate of a country if half of its population depends on freebies on one hand and well-educated and skilled are emigrating with a plan to save up for years on the other hand?!"

"Mere grandiloquent phrases cannot turn a tawdry lie into truth!"

◈

"A natural line of vertical and horizontal communication among the members of a family should debouch from the hearts and lead to acceptable solutions!"

◈

"Skilled technicians and personnel are merely enough to intimidate the enemy nation for it are more than a country vaunting its military strength to do this purpose!"

◈

"When the winds shift to a prograde direction, implementation of the preconceived ideas becomes easier -- in all walks of life!"

◈

"When some people realise that their boasting is sensed by whom the message is intended, they excuse that they brag for a cause and not

for themselves!"

"Param Vir Chakra is such a great honour that the legacy of valour and bravery of great soldiers continues to endure in the form of posthumous commemoration!"

"Communicating ideas is an art -- when the ideas reach out to the target audience, they would certainly develop into a material force!"

"Buddha said that if your compassion does not include yourself, it is incomplete. Yes, we should think of largesse only if our garden furnishes far more of our victuals!"

"The eolian caves formed by powerful winds make it difficult to clear off the sediments -- so will be the case of dugouts caused by negative thoughts!"

"Identifying contenders that don't have ulterior motives is the primary responsibility of an electorate!"

"Many hinterland students excel in their scholastics even though they find very scanty resources!"

"Despite their strong intuitional support, often people are forced to capitulate their resistance, with an adversary, or hopelessness before an irresistible opposing force!"

"Strong guts are impetrated to allow a tyro to take charge while keeping aside the most experienced!"

"Even though the opinions are poles asunder, the team that has a helluva ego would always try to win over the other -- forgetting that a fool only wins an argument!"

"Social Media platforms a battle of not only the Brainiac but also Manic!"

"Corporate funding to political parties leads to definite cronyism -- resulting in untoward decisions by the government to hive off the nationalised industries to private enterprises!"

"The real capacity of a balloon could be endured when it is distended due to the filling of air. In a similar vein, the mind's capacity could be discerned by infusing more knowledge into it!"

"Even the death cannot whisk away the incandescent vitality effectuated by an individual -- because of the best indentures!"

"I wonder why protesters do not realise that the property they mangle is the public property -- owned by the nation!"

"It leads to great dismay if a lucrative reward is expected even before making an effort and that attempt would turn into a futile endeavour!"

"Some political coalitions could be rightly seen as ludicrously acquiescent -- yesterday's all criticisms become approbation, overnight!"

◈

"The apotheosis of anything is a relative term. So, it cannot be held as a static feature as long as the inclusive variables decide on!"

◈

"There is a dire need to amend the constitution and rescind various clauses that are levelling off the talent in people in achieving their goals and forcing them to adjust with domestic law!"

◈

"Life is so unpredictable that our spirits take a sudden nosedive bowing to the upshot yielded by situational dénouement!"

◈

"The unswerving devotion, punctuality and discipline are the key elements needed for the effective administration!"

◈

"No sooner the world becomes fully dependent on the information superhighway than people would forget how otherwise the lives would have been!"

◈

"Acting naturally upon instinct and trying to be spontaneous are two mutually contradictory traits -- two knives cannot be accommodated in one sheath!"

◈

"Oftentimes, the contraband searches undertaken by the authorities would result in more creative methods of concealment and smuggling!"

"Rendition of fugitives is very essential as a training curriculum -- to prevent any pursuit of fugitives in warfare!"

CHAPTER SIX

Musings 6

"Change is inevitable and we need to espouse all genuine changes. Nonetheless, all orthodox practices cannot be marked down as practices of antediluvian times that behest a change!"

"Dissemination of the fake news on Social Networking Sites amounts to a breach of law. Nonetheless, people foolhardy flout those laws of the land!"

"Communication is the élan vital for the survival of the human race!"

"It's a common observation that the introvert people prefer seclusion and choose to live an austere life!"

"The creation on the earth is so wonderful that the prehensile tails in some animals capacitate them to lay hold of branches of trees!"

"Soldiers and farmers are the backbones of the nation. It would amount to a moral crime to vilify these fraternities -- who are always with the unknown you!"

◆

"Inventing oneself and what one can do is one of the best characteristics of doyens of every field!"

◆

"The focus in Indian marriages has now shifted to wearing of gaudy costumes and arranging exalted parties than according gravity to the decorum of nuptial knot!"

◆

"Everyone is correct in their one way. So, to keep up a cordial relationship, there's a need to pay healthy respect to the principles of comity!"

◆

"If an upheaval cannot be foreseen by states, it would more than likely presage the worst scrape -- one of the dreadful lessons taught by the Corona Times!"

◆

"We live peacefully by dint of the soldiers who safeguard the boundaries uniformly amidst both gelid and scorching temperatures!"

◆

"Social Networking Sites have paved a way for the launch of digital missiles of opprobrium -- at each other by politicians, without much effort!"

◆

"In this world of precarious jobs that demand robotic rendering by humans, the convalescence after great suffering has turned out to be unthinkable!"

◆

"Satmass Media can be comprehended as an extension lead of anthroposemiotics -- the field devoted to understanding the way humans communicate!"

"The so-called leaders always have a fear that frank and bold people could endanger their ascendancy, and for that reason, they prefer to have the company of unworthy shallow sycophants!"

"The value of some precious metals get tarnished temporarily due to verdigris. Similarly, some incidents may blemish the image of great people of the genre; but it won't last for a longer time!"

"The twilight is ephemeral -- ultimately it should get died into the dark!"

"It's a mandatory desideration that extremely conservative views have to be considered to avoid polarisation among members on significant issues -- otherwise it impacts the overall development of the state!"

"The protagonists of Indian movies are not less than any invincible Griffin!"

"The democracy would stay in doldrums until the time the nation remains aping the monarchy and keep awarding the lucrative positions to flatterers of the ruling party!"

"If ruling parties choose to stay corporate-friendly, follow the prerogative and neglect such priority sectors as agrarian, then it won't be a surprise to see their imminent debacle!"

"Though the new year celebrations seem to exude the unpropitious sitch created by Corona, the locus of contestation among the people still revolves around the same for some more time!"

"The voluminous writings must so have a good deal of the background -- attached to pioneering work!"

"If the best BGM of a movie is reprised at regular intervals in the movie plot, it rejuvenates the moods of the audience and leaves behind a wondrous feeling!"

"These days, trying to impart moral values through lectures is feckless -- because -- the concern is mere Vieux jeu!"

"The inscriptions from the period of emperor Ashoka are not only an apologia for the war but also the greatest revelations of his observations made during the Kalinga war!"

"Work-life balance is the only probable solution to dissociate from realities of modern life -- excessively loaded by stress-accompanied by fear of unknown and despondency!"

"If not the sword, the pommel of the sword should do its purpose!"

◈

"All those who can perceive the difference between a nest and a cage can also sense the difference between passion and compulsion!"

◈

"A pleasant smile on a comely face exudes an inexorable sparkling charm!"

◈

"A powerful pugilist aims for a knockout -- not just a mere win!"

◈

"The human beings need to learn from the Eusocial Insects that demonstrably develop large and multigenerational congregations!"

◈

"If the zest to hold a weapon is fulfilled, the terrorists would tend to use the weapon amok -- forgetting the humanitarian values!"

◈

"The longest lockdown ever has proven that even the paradise could turn into a hellhole!"

◈

"There's no doubt that one wacky idea that came from the mind of Arthur C Clarke has triggered many space scientists, resulting in the possibility of extraterrestrial relays!"

◈

"Ipso facto, at one or other point of time, a crime will be ratified -- because -- every criminal unintentionally leaves behind a clue!"

◈

"Sometimes, it is very difficult to use phonetic values in English -- it sounds pedantic if insisted on the exact pronunciation as that of a native speaker!"

"Emojis made it possible to exchange haptic stimuli over the social media to ersatz various emotions!"

"There is a thin line between being loyal and exhibiting integrity as to being hard-working but annoyingly servile!"

"Even the rubber has to be vulcanised before it attains a proper form then why do humans want to meet fame overnight?"

"To convey one's bowing thanks very effusive, the smile becomes wider and eyes get wet -- the communication by other means!"

"The present-day political debates do not even follow a modicum of decorum!"

"It has long been conjectured that there exists another world -- another solar system!"

"Once meet the power, the politicians get mired in gulosity and superciliousness!"

"Some war researchers could use the inscriptions on the sarcophagus for a better understanding of the warfare of that period!"

"To become an effective participant of a political debate, the major qualities one should have are ad hominem and ability to hurl personally targeted taunts -- to undertake bullying in the discussion room!"

"It's not that soldiers are insouciant about their lives ... it's their integrity towards the nation that makes them ever ready for sacrifices!"

"It is the obeisance of prevailing rules that creates the ability to control a matter in either way!"

"The story of each fallen warrior should be hailed to be u transpired inspiration for future generations -- it's not everyone's cup of tea to be a warrior!"

"The virtual groups of itinerant fraudsters are highly skilled social engineers -- wandering well nigh around to use various social engineering tools!"

"Efforts are required to raise warriors but not parasites -- the latter can happen obviously without any effort!"

"Social media are surging in the media world due to its significant characteristics -- ubiquity and interactivity!"

"A conflict is nothing but the means to put thousands of lives in jeopardy!"

◈

"Before an imagination turns into a reality, preparing for the success would be so exciting, albeit nerve-racking!"

◈

"When the time has its ruling, there would be no other choice but to retrocede the power back to the rightful owners!"

◈

"Satmass revolution, the technological advancement through satmass media, is a valuable tool by which people might future-proof themselves!"

◈

"If policy changes are undertaken without due deliberations, they might sometimes be proven costly and ineffective nostrum!"

◈

"In the beginning, many conceptual ideas crop up with esoteric significance. Nonetheless, they meet phenomenal recognition once their impact is felt!"

◈

"It's a common observation that people become quite a gadabout to relatives' homes to impress them and to have their support in times of dire straits. But such unfocused investment may not work always!"

◈

"If gatekeepers are not mandated, social media platforms would pavé a way for relentless netizens to acquire and practice the untoward quisling!"

◈

"It is not the external looks of an individual that counts but the prepossessing internal talent!"

"It's the mistakes that can be absolved; but not the blunders!"

"So far defeat is an unfamiliar entity for me — each effort etched on my memory from being a state ranker to an established author — an instinct somewhere in between cocky and confidence!"

"At times we feel like giving up in despair as our thoughts take on a situation like the sere stubble fields getting brooded in glamour!"

"Let someone be a bellwether of trends! But the followers should not be blinded by the light of irrational beliefs and practices thus set!!"

"For some best bib and tuckers, being a ragamuffin is a being not different from an animal — their actions speak louder than words in this regard!"

\- Sunday, 7 February, 2021, 10:45:44 AM

"History has never created exemplars rather exemplars have created the history!"

"Let the strumpets become Magdalen, but the history associated with the past would not be wiped off!"

"When personal experiences belie the truth, we need to comprehend the hidden wisdom in those experiences and consider it as the only truth!"

"Before any crucial decision is made final, the competent authority needs to consider the caveat in the proposal!"

"It's definite that a voracious reader could be an established author too!"

"The pleasure of venturing out into open fields on a beautiful and clear night to gawk at the galaxy and nebula is inexplicable!"

"The research reports should minutely limn the findings at the end even though by very nature research reporting is exhaustive!"

"Let the situation be prothalamion or elevation of the protagonist, the musical melody of Ilayaraja adds a decisive euphony!"

"Despite the best valiant media efforts, at times the results are underwhelming!"

"Certain economic policies make us feel that we are tightly locked in an indissoluble embrace -- leave no other option than going with the flow!"

"A leader's reputation is governed by the associates he keeps -- the unworthy toadies would diminish the repo and nullify the prevailing record of service to the community!"

"The avowed purpose of any editorial is to tweak the noses of the malfunctioning establishments!"

"The musical melodies inexplicably serve as anodyne that gives relief from everyday tensions and worries !"

"Indian traditional folk media is nearly an extinct genre. However, this format of media perdure in the guise and transformed form in each new media platform!"

"It is very difficult to meet a stature in a society wherein external factors like a bribe, recommendations, etc play a role -- even though the inherent talent is recognised among certain cognoscenti!"

"One of the concepts widely used by Artificial Intelligence is retargeting, wherein computers do all the work to figure out the individual requirements!"

"Palpably, an individual in any profession whose bailiwick is the comfort of other people, instead of self, is inclining and significant!"

"It is not hard to fathom the reason for a mightier Air Force role in modern warfare!"

"Each nation should design its policies according to the country's requirements. Nonetheless, if a third world nation tries to implement the policies adopted by a developed nation without much examination, such enforcement would be proven slipshod at best!"

"A masterpiece is carved after so much effort and if that does not receive much appreciation, the obvious feeling would be that we should have skipped the whole megillah!"

"If someone forgives a person and decides to not confront the controversial comments just because of deference to the person who made such comments, it should not be considered as his inability to defend!"

"Empathy and honesty are hidden traits among the highly sensitive people along with other noticeable characteristics as the spirit of the high-strung, petulant and spleenful sort!"

"Soon after attaining the reins, those who have starved for power for years would devour every soupcon of opportunity in the catch sight of!"

"Frequent violation of an armistice, agreed by neighbouring nations during the courtly venerated times, would certainly lead to massive warfare!"

"Social media are ubiquitous societal contaminants of considerable persistence!"

◆

"The successful people are those who deal deftly as the situation demands -- using an umbrella that best suits the situation while keeping aside ethics and morals that have a trivial value in the present-day society!"

◆

"If being orthodox means abhorring the downtrodden, as conceptualised by a few, then such faith is at the dyke -- there arises a need to comprehend the true meaning of Benign Providence of Sanatana Dharma!"

◆

"The consumers of mainstream media are often left with generic news content that emphasizes titillation, sensational events, and politically safe topics!"

◆

"How worldly-wise the system's design may be, the reason for the unforeseen outage is likely to have something beyond the designer's control!"

◆

"The ballet that best suits the music is not a mere divertissement -- it's a form of communication by other means!"

◆

"Everything undertaken by an air warrior becomes a mission -- its accomplishment with integrity and excellence is the very aim of such an air warrior, whose DNA is avowedly patriotism!"

◆

"The vanguard and luminaries of every sphere have established their charisma by giving their best -- not by flattering as parasites and

claiming the credits of others!"

"The comprador has changed their modus operandi from generation to generation -- otherwise their only purpose is mortgaging the stability of nations!"

"The uncannily prescient experiments would be ended up proving true!"

Musings 7

"The straight man having noble ideologies is always seen bent!"

"Truth, in my opinion, is a relative term -- usually what we believe in becomes the truth!"

"My observation in working with any organisation has it that the one who works sincerely is the same as of the least respected -- the inkling is any way they work!"

"If you start criticising yourself, you stop criticising others!"

"Situations become difficult only with the fear of facing them -- fear is the prime governor of combating the situation!"

"There's a thin line between grieving about something and thinking about something -- while the former leads to depression, the latter results in the solution!"

"The feeling of what people think of you makes you less confidant!"

◈

"We can govern our thoughts but not our emotions!"

◈

"Insecurity begins with the fear of losing something!"

◈

"The world one knows would come to an end the moment he breathes his last!"

◈

"The contemporary society, to me, seems just like the palace of moving cadavers -- everything looks artificial!"

◈

"One needs to be talented enough to distinguish between arrogance and self-respect, for there's a very thin line between!"

◈

"At times it becomes very difficult to bring out the exact emotions of the director in camera angles -- so is the case with an author! "

◈

"Wisdom is the ability to know the truth!"

◈

"Some writings make you understand the content while others let you attempt to comprehend what the author intends to convey!"

◈

"It is easier said than practising to face the fears and push through them!"

◈

"With conviction, people could indeed make plans but whether or not they would be effective depends on fate!"

"I have strappingly accepted it as true that people respect the opulence one acquired and not the individual himself!"

"Unfortunately the SWOT analysis has become the acid test for making friends and maintenance of relationships among the people!"

"There's no need to test the whole of an ocean to estimate its characteristics of it -- a mere single drop suffices the purpose!"

"It is a naturally evolving process that all butterflies undergo systematic metamorphosis. To mature into an adult, they pass through four stages of evolution — each stage has a different goal. Though it is not strictly talked about, I intensely believe that human lives also pass through such stages of evolution!"

"Want to take an acid test of friendship? just act as if you are no longer useful -- results just follow within no time!"

"Having an odious past is not that bad but the future does!"

"The country wherein small sector of taxpayers are fleeced heavily to offer freebies to the large sector wouldn't progress!"

"Mostly the reunions among old pals are full of treacle -- even the most serious persons to get teary-eyed!"

"Very wisely some celebrities cover up their inane malapropisms -- an art only a few can master!"

"Among the passel of unworthy employees, the worthy turns into an odd man out!"

"Only those who can spontaneously ad-lib on stage would be established as successful performers!"

"For any political party, how to propitiate the worst situation after a distressing defeat is an ever-burning question!"

"Empty nest syndrome is very hard to cope with!"

"It is better not to have prominent resolutions which constitute the basis of the greatest compromise, for compromise makes a good umbrella but a poor roof!"

"Evocation is high-priced!"

"The musical melodies give soporific effect!"

"The contemporary worldwide politics give vent to demagogues and not potential leaders!"

◈

"For whatsoever reasons, if the original manuscript is truncated to a reasonable length, the original flavour lasts!"

◈

"If there is a possibility of the existence of aliens, then there could be a definite likelihood of wormholes too!"

◈

"Many public speakers, mostly politicians, often bemuse being funny with being facetious!"

◈

"The pandemic time has reconciled the people's thinking about roistering celebrations!"

◈

"At workplaces, mostly employees feign busy when an unexpected and urgent work pop-up!"

◈

"The righteous people alone would never try to obfuscate their true solicitude!"

◈

"Success doesn't always come from hoity-toity educational institutions!"

◈

"Most of the workplace respects and greetings are merely smarmy -- probity is abstruse!"

"In line with my philosophies, when it is fortuitous to offer feedback, one must make the most of it. It's how organisational advancement and transformations surface!"

"The destitution that one passes through would make sure that the close relatives and friends move away from that person!"

"Gurus are the human derricks for the success of students!"

"The nation needs commodious ideologues and not the politics of prestidigitation!"

"The best example to reiterate that money rules the world is -- even during this pandemic, people forgot that currency notes too can be fomites!"

"One of the adamantine prejudices is that a person with a milquetoast personality could never be an adroit kingpin!"

"Human brain is so powerful that any powerful insult kindled is rankled in the mind forever!"

"We need to have virtual palisades to steer clear of the unsolicited intruders into the mind!"

"The inertia of reclusive calmness needs a great spur in life to reinstate the original state!"

"How could a nation take a progressive path when its voters have a flippant responsibility?!"

"Until and unless the workplaces are very congenial to its stakeholders, it turns strenuous to meet the desired results!"

"The political parties huckster the freebies as soon as the election approaches!"

"The contemporary Indian culture has the adventitious roots!"

"Even though the lugubrious end of Lata Mangeshkar's musical odyssey made the audience teary-eyed, she will be remembered forever as the only female nightingale that ever sang -- considering the very fact that it's the male nightingale that sings!"

"In Armed Forces, everything is scheduled in advance and the implementation goes as per the delineated plan!"

"Some movies imprint a very respectable colophon in our mind's title page about the theme of the movie?"

"At times, calmness is felt as startling as it could be!"

"All my teachers had a panache of teaching style -- though earnest in their teaching role!"

"The invaluable struggle of soldiers paves a way for civilians' outlay of time with their families -- the datum is appreciated by a very few people!"

"Insofar as picking up the check of a soldier is allowed, many people remember soldiers only when they need their support!"

"A prosperous marriage requires falling in love many times -- always with the same person!"

"Unexpectedness is thy name of life!"

"Every uniform is designed in such a way that it gives a restful appearance on those who wear -- along the lines of the purpose of their operation!"

"Taking one's baby for the first time into hands is probably the best anxiety one could ever experience -- because -- it gives the fretfulness speckled with hope and enclosed with love!"

"Indubitably, along with the many magnificent emotions, novel parents experience while huddling their new babies for the first time, comes a bit of terror and a bit of dread. Being responsible for the life of

a tiny human forever and always is not an easy task!"

◆

"Overwhelming, exhausting and terrifying are the three words that could describe the new fatherhood!"

◆

"It is impossible to gaze into the face of a tiny infant without feeling a rush of joyful emotions!"

◆

"Nothing can become more central to the mother in front of her child's welfare -- taken together, it's after all mother's love that cannot surpass anything in this world!"

◆

"When things won't happen as desired, so many unpleasant judgements vacillate in the mind!"

◆

"The greatest punishment one can have is to become vexatious oneself for being up the creek to serve his parents when they need care for their geriatric needs!"

◆

"Adjusting between two dissimilar lives could be grim because it could sense like neither community recognises the other!"

◆

"My experience had it that what may be an expected communication style for a defence person may be frustrating to a civilian, and vice versa!"

◆

"If anyone asks me what I have done to make my life worthwhile, without any second thought I will respond with a good deal of pride and fulfilment that I am an air veteran!"

"Mission and men are two fundamental elements of true leadership!"

"The astute observations drawn from the most successful people will be of great inspiration to the next generation!"

"Although set in the period immemorial, Vedas reflect the feelings and zeitgeist of contemporary society!"

"I have never seen a healthy discussion among different leadership rather than being excessively captious!"

"I do keep many things at the back of my mind when I write my own palindrome words or phrases!"

"When we read through a story, our analysis should consider both the antithetical forces of good and evil in the story!"

"Rarely we find any book that could be considered as a literary tome!"

"The best teacher uses euphemisms wisely to make every student understand what exactly he intends to convey!"

◈

"If the top brass is sanguine about the success of the team, nothing can stop them from motivating their teams to achieve the best results!"

◈

"Every stola and toga has become a point of discussion -- mere wastage of valuable time!"

◈

"It's always the winsome personalities that become the centre of the attraction!"

◈

"I often observe that few people who don't deserve a position they hold but have been bestowed with responsibilities for whatsoever reason, ramble non-sequitur comments that aren't logical!"

◈

"It's the patriotism of soldiers that results in their derring-do activities against adversaries!"

◈

"Freebies are a sort of juggernaut in the arsenal of every stakeholder that wants to reign!"

◈

"Occasional quips in a speech attract the audience -- an art of eminent orators!"

◈

"The journey of success is a ziggurat with so many steps, having the final step as the goal!"

◈

"The ideologies of true visionaries can never be myopic!"

◈

"Being obsequious can sometimes be not less than any slavery -- though there's a thin line in between!"

◈

"The desired results can't be achieved if peremptory innuendo becomes the final resolve!"

◈

"A very good film script could turn into an utter flop due to poor screenplay and slapdash editing!"

◈

"A good mentor always hews closely to the very objective of his mentee's research work!"

◈

"It's the confidence given by in-depth knowledge of the subject that makes a person address audiences with a nonchalant ease!"

◈

"It's an obvious thing that almost everyone experiences the same nervousness on their first attempt, but they rarely speak with candour about that anxiety!"

◈

"An idea and action always work in tandem -- solus neither works!"

◈

"Success does not only mean one's win, it can also be viewed as the opponent's failure!"

◈

CHAPTER EIGHT

Musings 8

"Irrefutably, technology has long been a lashing influence behind advancements in communication. Nonetheless, contemporary technologies are profoundly altering the manner of human communication!"

"From employment to economy, and from warfare to peace communication, Artificial Intelligence is transforming the nature of every aspect of human life. However, there's a dilemma associated with Artificial Intelligence -- whether it is advancing towards this planet into a better place to live or a place full of disaster!"

"Insofar as war reporting is concerned, holding a pen is as daring as holding a gun. So, the media people should understand their responsibilities and appreciate that the line between activism and journalism is at times thin!"

"Effective Communication is the greatest weapon that alone can transform the world into a better place to live!"

"With the changing times, we also need to change -- the same inherited rules from the colonial era cannot be enforced even in this era

of Satmass Media for the reason that it amounts to social deprivation!"

"In the case of communication for palliative care, technology can be suitably applied to turn the discussions into an exceedingly collaborative form of communication over the Internet and smartphones!"

"I often find political leaders pontificate even on the most sensitive issues -- without ever thinking about the aftermath of their statements!"

"Unfortunately, most of those who lead people today are those irascible cranks that never have a kind word for any of the warriors from the Tri-forces!"

"When the true colours of a leader are made public, then the showtime begins wherein the leader tries to dissemble his responses!"

"Gift of gab and a marked talent for extemporaneous speaking is one of the finest personality attributes! "

"A person need not be formally educated to judge humans with a confident and gayly trenchant way -- mere personal experience is more than sufficient!"

"Certainly it is better to restrain oneself from committing a blunder than opting to coax someone after the irreparable damage takes place!"

"Once we comprehend that an argument is untenable from an intellectual, moral and practical standpoint, it's better to surrender!"

"Prefer to refuse to let others do your thinking - just respect and use your brain and instinct!"

"The greatest philosophy has it that one should not do those things to others, the same things that we expect others to not do to us!"

"Indubitably, in this world of the survival of the fittest, until the end of time, there will be an incessant veiled fightback for supremacy!"

"Nowadays it is very difficult to find people with a rectitudinous character and a spotless record!"

"Education is not a diurnal service that can not be bought just in the souk. Nonetheless, the present education has made it possible!"

"Fundamental change can be brought about to eliminate all sorts of discrimination through the learning of human rights as a way of life!"

"A person is not assessed the same by any two people-- if one person finds a pleasant smile and ready compliment, another might experience oleaginous demeanour!"

"The only solution to raise the confidence levels of chapfallen people is --effectual communication!"

"A war plan should essentially include an annexed plan of strategic communication for it would devise a game plan that would ultimately lead towards winning of the conflict!"

"Artificial Intelligence is facilitating people to approach creative activities in a manner that bears a resemblance to Mathematics -- muddling the line between art and science!"

"There's no doubt that the present-day political system is revolving around cronyism -- crony capitalism and crony journalism!"

"In my opinion, regardless of a predominant robust law to prevent sexual harassment in India, we never had real discussions -- it has been a mere cloak-and-dagger!"

"Ideologically in any given nation, true loyalists do not serve some imagined unchallengeable unit called nation or country; rather, they serve the needs and aspirations of every person!"

"The impact of Social Media on sleep patterns is a topic of great attention given the recognized adverse effects of sleep deprivation on health!"

◆

"Tolerance is a philosophy most of us live by, which makes us recognize that education is the key to the promotion of peace!"

"Ignorance about cultural, religious and ethnic diversity present in the world can lead to diffidence. With education, however, there can be a better understanding of different customs and beliefs!"

"Only such an educational system can work well in future that imbibes moral values among the children and youth!"

"Politics is the decisive game of sales -- selling an idea to the public while the politician attempts to sell oneself!"

"Yes, it's not everyone's cup of tea to be a soldier! Nonetheless, we can all come together to support the families of the soldiers who laid down their lives for the sake of the nation!!"

"It's a matter of fact that India lacks a comprehensive strategic response to terrorism--there is a need to have an all-inclusive code to counter-terrorism for the reason that most of our reactions are imprudent!"

"Albeit surrounded by so many difficulties in military jobs, many women still find that they thoroughly enjoy their jobs in the military while they serve the nation with zeal and dedication!"

"There is no other force that could change the temperaments of individuals than the inherent vigour. A change has to come from within!"

"If there is a social problem, one should try to attend to it by offering some sort of amicable solution to remove it rather than instigating other means that eventually land up in violence and offer a threat to the nation's security!"

"A thriving project finishing point depends on many aspects. Communication is the most significant one. A person or institution can't go wide of the mark if they formulate a lot of exertion to communicate the most excellent they can!"

"At this crucial time of the pandemic, when the black clouds gathered in the welkin, the Almighty has chosen his best creations to serve the people!"

"I would like to assert that there is a binding criterion required for getting elected to the legislative institutions i.e. to be well-heeled. Is it not a point to ponder?"

"The ongoing total lockdown period due to Covid 19 has at least not left us being held incommunicado!"

"While at work everyone wants to stay back at home and people during lockdown wish they go back to work. It seems that this is the trick of the light that alters the intensity of the viridity. Oh, we always want what we haven't got!"

"At a time when there is a dire need for the entire nation to join hands together, the quixotic view of government by the opposition is not appreciated!"

"Can we let the present phase of time be an age of laissez-faire... absolutely no, for the reason that the world is full of irresponsible idiots who need a continuous reminder!"

"Out of the numerous connotations arise ideals and institutions. Nevertheless, these ideals and institutions are valuable only insofar as they support the fulfilment of each and everything!"

"Mass media messages, the source of heuristics, are congregating on one aspect of the situation created by the Covid-19 virus while ignoring other siqnificant aspects!"

"The philosophical belief is that people are born with a purpose. I extend this thought to other inert existences too -- certain things have arisen to a definite drive!"

"A battle does not take place only on the battlefield but sometimes in the public domain too. The result of winning or losing would be, thus, decided in the court of public opinion!"

"I often wonder why people scarcely speak until the time something out blazes massively!"

"Advancements in technology mean nothing if the system like manual scavenging still prevails in countries like India!"

"Likewise, like we have the Internet as one of the few positive bequests of cold war terror, we should have such ideal inheritances that follow-on era of the pandemic Corona!"

"The people who are always been a bit of a maverick are the only individuals enjoying the lockdown for the reason that there's no change for them!"

"Social media, an informal medium of communication, can lead to an equally casual attitude to grammar. But the truth is that social media is great for word nerds -- provides a rich playing field for experimenting with developing and subverting language!"

"Social media-driven participatory communication has allowed people to become the subjects of their development and not simply objects of technology or process!"

"As social media continues to permeate various issues, the legislative institutions are also forced to post official content on social media platforms!"

"Facing a situation of adversity is an art, not a science!"

"Human beings need a medium to communicate emotions, instinctive or intuitive feeling as distinguished from reasoning or

knowledge!"

◈

"The pandemic Corona that resulted in a never seen lockdown is causing hypnagogic hallucinations, the regularly petrifying acuities!"

◈

"Social media, in my opinion, is a stringent wonder of wonders that has in operation become an ingrained and important part of our everyday lives!"

◈

"Even a canard is latent to get deflagrated when it is just allowed to get an initial thrust! "

◈

"The basis of a wonderful technological invention is a mere imagination, which is indistinguishable from magic!"

◈

"Gratitude will swing to a higher rate of recurrence for enticing much better things!"

◈

"Non-verbal communication rules over verbal communication. It is not just regurgitating a cliché. It's my honest conviction!"

◈

"Intelligence has a definite survival value. Nonetheless, it can take the sides of both good and evil"

◈

"It is very unfortunate to note that the rebellious and stupid youth have no regret for their peccant behaviour during this lockdown period!"

"The nation-states need an intense colloquy, involving stakeholders from several areas, to decide on the next course of action to eradicate the pandemic Corona!"

"The lockdown in many countries has been ineffectual due to a few adamant citizens' obstinate and perverse refusal to understand the significance of such an imposition!"

"The present situation offers two possibilities: either we educate the reckless people adequately or we should not. Both are equally petrifying!"

"It is the mark of adamant to obliterate something better for humankind because they cannot comprehend the good!"

"There's a thin but significant line between the obiter dicta of human judges and the laws of nature. In the first case, the resulting judgement may have some mercy. Nonetheless, in the second case, there won't be any chance of appeal!"

"The present situation created by pandemic Covid-19 is a territorial striptease for the planet of abundance!"

"The dead noonday heat had even stilled the songs of the birds. Nonetheless, during this lockdown period amidst such adverse climatic conditions, we still find rogues roaming around!"

"In the name of further evolution, our culture and traditions are ambitious to oblige the unsolicited progression -- resulting in the obliteration of the entire global village! "

"Indubitably, if a person seems disingenuous, it's better to infer that the person is not genuine and thereby avoid association with that person!"

"It is very fateful that the people, who are drawn in the noble services at some stage in this phase of the crisis caused by the pandemic Covid-19, are socially ostracized by the communities due to the fear of the unknown!"

"The fear of the unknown is a threat to the conducive progression!"

◆

"The language of politicians is often disparagingly referred to as gratuitous slang ... for it is specific to the political fraternity!"

◆

"It is very strenuous to understand the eccedentesiast because such people never communicate openly about how they feel! "

◆

"Both traditional and social media have palpably emerged as important institutions of mediation in the contemporary world societies and have thus transformed political communication networks!"

◆

"I wonder how could a person, who is supposedly relying on freebies, can spend exorbitantly on liquor!"

◆

"I surmise that if a person chauffeurs someone out of humanity if be treated as a chauffeur, would make that humanity put off to find a place in burial ground!"

◆

"Life is so unpredictable-- once again proved by bereavements caused by the sudden and unforeseen disaster through the spread of gas from a chemical factory in Visakhapatnam -- ultimately subdued the damage caused by Covid-19!"

◆

"There's a dire need for the paradigm shift in the areas allied to disaster management!"

◆

"I consider the opening of wine shops during lockdown period while tea shops remain closed is unquestionably verboten!"

◆

"Everything can be gilded in this universe, except for mother's love -- because -- it's invariably available only in the purest form!"

◆

"Even though soldiers too are only human, they own remarkable skills in handling weapons and safeguarding people. Their contributions to the nation are to be aggrandized... not just appreciated!"

◆

"Death knell when reverberated from all sides would tender the only offer, fatality. Nation-states are encountering such a situation in

combating COVID-19!"

"When the best ideologies fail to survive amidst foolish decisions, it is impelled to accept the conviction that man is meagre flotsam and jetsam in the river of destiny!"

"It is palpable that humans are creators of wonderment. Nonetheless, when it comes out to be an act of God, they give up the ghost -- thus accentuating the very fact that there's some supernatural power beyond the reach of man! "

"When passion becomes one's profession, the capitulated results are of epitome elegance. Of course, it is not just regurgitating a cliché rather it's my sincere belief!"

"It is a diffident act that the soldiers are always ready to relinquish their comfortable lives, fighting for the country to safeguard the people they don't even know. There is no doubt that it involves a lot of valour and humanity!"

"Even petite gravel becomes paramount when you are alone and surrounded by some stray dogs that jump out of the circumambient air -- indicates that everything has its importance!"

"What if the mind's mirror that reflects the unvarying you, itself calls for your past contemplation!?"

"The universe has survived opulence and grandiosity after every disaster, ergo the universe is certainly bodacious!"

"From time to time, even the exiguous repast to its maximal crumb offered out of benevolence would make it as gratifying as viable!"

"Social media is indubitably a neoteric revolution of communication, ergo it allows everybody becoming a partaker in the discussions. Nevertheless, every so often the feeds make the participants smirk or scratch their heads!"

"Marriage is quintessentially a communion of life -- an entirety about a weary loving communication between wife and husband!"

"Nowadays the media debates have become the platforms to preen the contenders themselves and their respective organisations, throughout the day!"

"After a few years, even the best book on and about Covid-19 will become the shaggy-dog story! "

"The incumbency of almost every nation has lurched the people to their fate amidst the worst circumstances resulting due to the pandemic Corona!"

"Music is a means of communication that provides vital sustenance of human interaction when explicit needs make other forms of communication difficult!"

am

CHAPTER NINE

Musings 9

"Known for her inherent resilience, India would assuredly overcome any ill-timed crisis. Nevertheless, a bit of preparedness is fit to impetrate!"

"As often as not, the best scripts get marred by illogical longueurs while even a poor script can become awe due to the invigorating stride of the main story!"

"The society that has a magnificent leadership commingled with maverick managerial transcendence would surpass in every walk of life!"

"Some individuals and places -- the august -- are not sought-after by their names but their entitled appellations!"

"Opinions based on the accepted wisdom of the people having considerable experience in the field would sometime be proven better than the methods that depend heavily on heuristic algorithms and statistical models!"

"The long-drawn-out lockdown has begotten obsession of the typical pandiculation activity!"

◈

"The stiction caused by the pandemic has kindled a discord made by prolonged disruption of life that compromised both quality and control!"

◈

"Illaiyaraja's music is irrefragable afflatus that sends a thrill down the spine and gets imprinted in the memory to make everyone melomaniac!"

◈

"I am confounded to note that many people are having no compunction about leaving their parents to their fate when they need geriatric support, but have so much involvement for their offsprings!"

◈

"People that make trenchant comments would have to often face a lot of criticism, even if those comments are about one of the eternal verities!"

◈

"Though my intentions have been just to succour the needy, most often I land up in the ditch of being used -- precisely because I am a little naive!"

◈

"People with extreme emotions are emotionally not intelligent -- for this reason, they are capricious, in general!"

◈

"Right person in the right place means designating a strong proponent of reform and transparency at the helm of affairs -- the reins

with cogency!"

"Collation of significant actions would give rise to the best concomitant, just like firing salvo yields the best results! "

"The near enough online classes can not stopgap the real classroom lectures for the reason that the former, over time, would turn into vanilla lectures and boring speeches!"

"It is precise that radio is the theatre of the mind because it signposts the serene ability, elegance, outfits, and methods by which radio performers mesmerise vibrant imagery in minds of their audiences with the help of only sound!"

"In line with my strong belief, great teachers would never vilipend or belittle the students for not being quick-witted!"

"It is onerous to manage the fissile core of the mind and control its rigid thinking! "

"The scams in India are much of a muchness to any whodunit set out ordeal by ordeal!"

"I am not acquainted with cutting and running away from moral responsibilities, lest I would have divagated from the fated path and overcome meanders in my life long back!"

"I have neither lost confidence in a benign Providence nor I would ever lose it -- my faith in the Indian credo and Sanatana Dharma is resolute!"

"Even the bellwether of economics would fail to prognosticate the ensuing situation of the global economy due to the extant pandemic, Covid-19!"

"The brave soldiers from the armed forces have laid down their lives to stand between the nation and oblivion even as the nation is facing the worst problem that it has ever seen before!"

"There is an increasing propensity to conflate the vested influence of the governing gentry with those of the state!"

"The stalwart patriotism exhibited by the soldiers safeguarding the nation has not only proved irresistible but is also ever commendable!"

"If you have a strong credence, there is no harm in being at odds -- because -- little later you could be proven a celebrated revisionist!"

"Retorting to the enemy's fomentation is technically and fairly masterful, but is fitfully distracting in its brilliance!"

"One of the most important aspects of communication is to determine the precise meaning of a word ... for that, it is very essential

to parse the sentence!"

"The colonial influence on Indians is so high that we pretermit events more or less exasperating to follow the urbane Englishman!"

"The military commander's stentorian roar of voice is enough to keep everyone in order!"

"The fear associated with big government benevolence is not less than any big business trust!"

"One should avoid the situation of getting deracinated by the employer just because of his reckless attitude and become jobless!"

"The best business skills often prerequisite legerdemain to make clients believe that they are getting the best deal!"

"Education alone is the exclusive Passepartout to many inconclusive issues!"

"Emulating the sturdy work ethic of a successful person to be triumphant would sometimes yield the desired results!"

"Those individuals whose intramural core values are mission, integrity and excellence, would be alone able to configure the critically important vanguard of a great workforce!"

◆

"People, who are conscientious to not shirk their duties, often do not believe in agreeable words and comforting lies!"

◆

"After a perpetuated hectic schedule, an immense sea of leisure would make us feel contented. Nevertheless, if the same continues, it might result in a succumbed situation to ennui and despair!"

◆

"It seems that the extreme social media agog among the masses made people lose their orbit of physical movement and contact with their fellow creatures!"

◆

"The existence of individuals has become so insipid and perfunctory that a frisson of excitement is lost in everyone's life!"

◆

"The memories associated with songs -- irrespective of whether galling or pleasing -- would take us back into sure and certain memories!"

◆

"Tribulations in life -- callings from God -- come as a bolt from the blue in combo packs, wrapped with personalised messages!"

◆

"Aesthetics, the inherent quality of any performing art, needs to be mastered with the greatest deftness to communicate what exactly is intended!"

◆

"Do felling prostrated before the idols while enkindling wickedness among fellow humans serves the very propose?!"

"I observe ever and anon people turn out to become magnanimous; and in a contemporaneous scenario, I see no reason why such good things should not go on and on persistently"

"It is true that God gives us many recollections to save us at condemnatory moments. Natch, our greatest affluence lies in identifying and scanning those anamneses!"

"The decisions made by a resolute mind are much more exacting and fastidious than those imprudent and exasperating parallels!"

"In seclusion when unsolicited thoughts surmount, the tunes of Illaiyaraja -- exquisite wonders of multiplication -- would grace ethereal somnolence!"

"Certain conversations make us pass through many stages from imprudence to impertinence and finally to ribaldry!"

"I think even the Gods grow jealous of too much contentment and show their displeasure, all of sudden, in various forms such as natural calamities or worst pandemics like Covid-19!"

"At times, even if it is desired to pass on some message full of resolve, the smothering lines may not be carried properly for obvious reasons!"

◆

"Incontestably, the power of effective communication can reinstate the strong faith as it shatters the obstinate lost hope in a person into pieces!"

◆

"When the nation needs the support, fitfully everyone throngs the highness, press on with the procession and excitedly talk about the bravery of soldiers; and within no time at full tilt people forget their services upon restoration of normalcy!"

◆

"My observation has it that a mild and complaisant person if pestered repeatedly may become exceedingly truculent or voluble!"

◆

"The lockdown period detested the whole business of many people and pervaded thoughts of throwing up their work to return to their native places!"

◆

"Too deep for words, often people land up in brevity in expressing the highest form of what is prepensed!"

◆

"If the time is propitious and favouring, even the distant relative draws nearer -- takes a jiffy somersault antithetically! "

◆

"Even though celebrities do possess a retinue of many servants, they do often faltered to their gaoler in the company or left to solitary confinement -- celebrity souls in the state of penance!"

◆

"The time has come wherein the universal populace has to become philosophical enough to accept nature's readjustments!"

"The dreary cycle of the morning, noon and night resulted from the prolonged lockdown due to pandemic covid-19 made human lives bland!"

"No one's life has ever been calm and Composed. It perpetually hops from one anxiety to another!"

"No regard for elders, precisely teachers, the younger generation of contemporary times sit high in a chair and don't even pay compliments … disregarding the fact that it would be blasphemous!"

"I wonder if a swill of toddy or liquor that drags a person into an inebriated state would mitigate the weariness of the body at the end of day's labour as claimed by many?!"

"Communication is a very powerful tool that even an intersperse with occasional monosyllabic comment gives significant feedback!"

"The more I read Indian philosophy, the more I started believing that It is futile to try to avoid what destiny has ordained!"

"If the time is propitious, everything goes in one's favour. Otherwise, the time has its game plan to prove its strength!"

"An individual continually indulging in facetious and tasteless remarks in congregation is haunted by an obdurate attitude!"

"At times, weighty words are necessary to convey the intended message. Nonetheless, it should be born in mind that sonorous words are liable to inflict pain!"

"Leading a spartan life would never drive one's forehead throbbed with the strain of concentration caused due to last-minute bustles!"

"It would be more honourable to die for the nation and rise to the rank of a hero than capitulate oneself to the enemy forces!"

"What does the hardened hunter care for if he hears the growling of a tiger or the roaring of a lion?!"

"In the Indian setting, many vital discussions crop up abominably during the meal! "

"Patriotism is beyond extremities -- has no fringe limits -- then why should people be patriotic on chosen occasions to spill seasonal patriotism?!"

"India has never reified autarky because of the depredations of the nation's wealth and resources -- either by colonial rulers or native business conglomerates!"

"Similar to the way rabbits vamoose before the entering of the ferret, the suborned beat a hasty retreat before the anti-corruption authorities take charge!"

"Most often many untrained people create exquisite mysteries of multiplication -- needless to say that some people are born with inherent talents!"

"Bygone was the time when teachers used to correct students by imposing physical punishments and students used to prepare their skins for the next day's pinching and caning!"

"The present situation for many people is -- the money in the bank is fast melting due to the unemployment...forcing to wear their feet out for employment!"

"My observation has it that some people are inept spending their time on unwanted things while others are professionally occupied -- just to extend their working hours for no valid reason!"

"Just like serpents shed their skin through sloughing for vivification, human beings need to come in for the notional sloughing for the rejuvenation of creative life force called rebirth, transformation, immortality and healing! "

"Besides focussing on the academic activities alone, schools -- the temples of personality development -- must inculcate a sense of noblesse oblige among its students!"

◆

"It is sometimes better to end a relationship without giving any warning of the volte-face rather than compromising for an extended time and suffer as a result! "

◆

"It is the legerdemain of the business planners that make customers believe that they get the best deal in town!"

◆

"Often, investigation reports in sensational cases are bowdlerised before they are promulgated to the media and public -- intentions can either be good or bad! "

◆

"It's better, to tell the truth, and all of it, without any subterfuge -- and repose thereafter -- rather than deceive the truth and sustain a shrouded fear!"

◆

"Even though there are laid down codes of ethics and moral conduct for every profession, many employees do not feel any guilty of their substantial dereliction of duty!"

◆

"Many stalwart authors are masterful in making readers getting into the scene of chronicling and laying hold of their deep concentration!"

◆

"Inordinately talented people are mostly full of meekness -- can rarely see an element of braggadocio in them!"

◆

"Shopping malls have impinged the business areas of small supply chains similar to the way snakes gatecrash anthills!"

◈

"To deliver the best, as opposed to the passing of pejorative comments, leaderships demand emboldening exposition cosseted by sustenance!"

◈

"One of the key factors that govern an individual's success is longanimity -- to cheer on for self despite repeated failures!"

◈

"These days journalists are making allusions to human interest stories that add an estival feel with unbearable heat to those stories!"

◈

"Any requite, might be an as simple one as an obligated smile, would have its greatest impact!"

◈

"Individuals who inveigh against the gratuitous have become a rare species -- the extinct class of human beings that learnt to compromise and not correct! "

◈

"The tutelage that comes up with the conservative people pops up fatuous stuff to present-day youngsters -- it is a mere rueful admiration and amusement to them!"

◈

"People who could assimilate things easily are docile in disposition -- can create wonders without a great toiling!"

◈

"In a serious attempt to write the history of the Tollywood Film Industry, there would be an unequivocal chapter on the heyday of Illaiyaraja -- the period of 1980s and 1990s!"

◆

"I wonder if this universe would ever have such leaders who could get the strikingly genuine plaudits of the people?!"

◆

"The research work that begins with an impregnable operational definition and hypothesis would patently knuckle under the best results!"

◆

"Though it's a known fact that one's opinions are often derided and held as bunkum, it is always better to take part in expressing the views rather than keeping tight-lipped!"

◆